BILLY'S
LEARNING
ADVENTURES

JONNETTA BINION

AuthorHouse™
1663 Liberty Drive
Bloomington, IN 47403
www.authorhouse.com
Phone: 1 (800) 839-8640

Published by AuthorHouse 07/12/2018

ISBN: 978-1-5462-5111-8 (sc)
ISBN: 978-1-5462-5110-1 (e)

Library of Congress Control Number: 2018908152

Print information available on the last page.

authorHOUSE®

Billy's First Day Of Kindergarten

Today is the first day of kindergarten for little Billy. He is excited for what he could learn in school. As Billy walks into school, he is greeted by his Principal Mr. Smith.

"Hello young man, welcome to Madison Elementary, what's your name?"

"Billy" he replied. Billy shook Mr. Smith's hand, then Mr. Smith asked with a smile, "what grade are you in Billy?" Billy replied with excitement "kindergarten!" Mr. Smith laughed with joy because of Billy being so excited and happy for his first day of school.

"Well then," Mr. Smith said, "Are you ready to learn what kindergarten is all about?" "Oh yes," Billy answered, "But I'm a little nervous."

"Oh, why is that Billy?" Mr. Smith asked. "Because I don't know what I will be learning" Billy replied. Mr. Smith kneeled down to see Billy eye to eye and said, "It is okay to be nervous Billy, believe me, everyone will be nervous and excited for their first day of school. For you," Mr. Smith replied, "You are going to adventure what school is all about in a fun and educational way."

"I like to have fun!" Billy said excitingly. "That is awesome" Mr. Smith said. The bell had rung, and Mr. Smith walked with Billy to his classroom.

When Billy walked into class, he was greeted by his teacher Miss. Rose.

"Hello Billy, my name is Miss. Rose, I am your kindergarten teacher, welcome to your classroom." "Nice to meet you Miss. Rose "Billy said.

"I have to get going, but it was nice speaking with you Billy ", Mr. Smith said. Before Mr. Smith left, he shook Billy's hand and said "If you ever feel you need to talk, you can always come see me in my office."

"Thank you, Mr. Smith," Billy said, and Mr. Smith left off to his office.

With a smile on her face, Miss. Rose guided Billy around the room to show him where he will be sitting. "You will be sitting here on the letter B."

"That's the first letter of my name" Billy said with excitement.

"That's right" Miss Rose replied, "Everyone will sit according to the first letter of their first name ".

"I'm going to my desk to get all the worksheets together for you and your classmates, maybe you would like to adventure around the room and meet everyone."

"But I don't know anyone here Miss Rose" Billy said nervously.

"That's okay Billy, everyone doesn't know each other here too, but that is what makes kindergarten so great" Miss Rose said, "because you can get to know them and become friends ". "Okay, I can do that" Billy said, and off he went to adventure with his classmates.

The first stop Billy made was at the tank surrounded by a little girl named Annie, and a little boy named CJ. Billy walked up to his classmates and said, "Hi, I'm Billy."

"Hi Billy, I'm Annie" "and I'm CJ" they both answered.

"Wow, that is a big turtle!" Billy said with excitement. "Her name is Mindy"

Annie said. "She is our class pet "CJ replied. Billy started having fun with CJ and Annie and adventured around the room with them. Billy noticed a lot of toys, stations, and pictures with a lot of colors. "Okay class," Miss Rose announced "time to start our lesson, please take a seat in your spot, and let's begin ".

Billy sat on the B, and noticed Annie on the A, and CJ on the C. They all laughed because they were together. As Miss Rose began the lesson, Billy thought to himself, "I think I'm going to have the best school year ever ".

Billy Learns The Alphabet

Since the first day of school, Billy was ready to take on the world of learning. One day in class, Billy was sitting at the table with his new friends Annie and CJ, with pencil in hand and paper, ready to learn. As soon as the bell rang, Miss Rose walked in. "Good morning class" she said. "Good morning" said the class.

"Today," Miss Rose said, "we will learn how to say and write our ABC's. We will learn with pictures. Each picture represents the first letter of the alphabet." Miss Rose then pulled out a deck of cards and gave one card to each student and kept the remaining. "First," she said, "I will sing the alphabet song, and then you all will sing along with me. A, B, C, D, E, F, G… H, I, J, K, L, M, N, O, P… Q, R, S. T, U, V…W, X, Y, and Z, now I know my A, B, C's, next time won't you sing with me." After Miss Rose sang the alphabet song, Billy and the other students sang along with Miss Rose. "A, B, C, D, E, F, G…H, I, J, K, L, M, N, O, P…Q, R, S. T, U, V. W, X, Y, and Z, now I know my ABC'S, next time won't you sing with me."

"Great job everyone" Miss Rose said. Billy was happy to sing such a great song. "Now each person will come up with their card and tell the class what card they have, and what letter the picture starts with. First up Annie." Annie walked up to the front and presented her card.

She had the picture of an apple, which starts with the letter A. "Great job Annie" Miss Rose said, "Billy, your next." Billy walked up to the front of the class and presented his card as well. "For my card I have a picture of a bear, bear starts with the letter B." "That's correct" Miss Rose said. Billy was so happy and proud of himself. After everyone finished their turn and showed their picture, Miss Rose went to the board to teach the children how to write. After writing and reciting all day it was time to go home.

As Billy was walking with Annie and CJ out the school doors, they were singing the alphabet song. "Today has been the best day ever" he said. "I can't wait to learn more again."

Billy Learns Math

Billy's experience in learning has made him so excited to go to school every day. In class Miss Rose was teaching the students math. "Okay everyone let's take out a pencil and paper write down these math problems. 1+1=, next 1+2=, 1+3=, 1+4=, 1+5=, 1+6=, 1+7=, 1+8=, 1+9=, and 1+10=." Miss Rose had the students write down each math problem right under the next. She then gave out blocks for the students to use to solve each problem.

"This is called addition," she said, "for addition, we find the total or sum by combining two or more numbers. With the blocks I gave you, I would like you all to use these to help you come up with the sum for each problem. Let's start with the first problem, 1+1. Now, take one block and place it in front of you," Miss Rose said, "and now take another block and place it next to the first block. How many blocks do you have? Billy?" "I have one, two. Two blocks" he answered. "That is correct" Miss Rose said. Billy smiled with joy.

After going through each problem Miss Rose reminded the children that blocks are always a good tool to use when doing all types of math. She then had to children pair up in groups to find the answer to the rest of the problems. After all the problems were complete everyone recited the answers.

After such a wonderful day of learning math Billy went home and practiced his addition with his own blocks. As he was counting, his mother walked by "1+1=2, 1+2=3, 1+3=4" Billy said. His mom smiled and said, "I'm so proud you," and went on her way.

Billy Learns His Colors

Billy loves to color. He even loves the colors he sees when it rains. One rainy day, Billy was stuck inside class because of the rainy weather. Even though it was raining outside Billy couldn't help but notice the lovely colors he sees out the window.

Miss Rose walked by. "Miss Rose," said Billy, "what are those colors I see outside, there so nice" he said. "That is a rainbow Billy, it is nice, maybe you will see a leprechaun" she said. Billy just laughed. "But what are the colors of the rainbow?" he asked. "That is a great question, what are the colors of the rainbow, to answer that I guess it's time to start our lesson".

Everyone went to their table and Miss Rose went to the front to grab her poster filled with many different colors and words. "On this poster we have many different colors, this color is **red**. Red is spelled R-E-D, red". The class then repeated after Miss Rose for every color she had on her board. The following colors were, **blue**, yellow, orange, green, brown, and **black**.

"Each color can stand alone or be mixed to make a color of your choice" said Miss Rose. "For instance, we could take the colors **blue** and yellow, to make the color green". Miss Rose took some paint that was yellow and **blue**, and mixed them together. Billy was amazed. Miss Rose then passed out a picture that the children had to color to make a rainbow.

"This is what I saw outside" said Billy. "That's very true" Miss Rose said. "I would like you all to color the rainbow the color it should be". They colored the **red**, orange, yellow, and the green. After completing their daily work, it was time to go home. As Billy stepped outside he could see the rain stop and the sun shining bright, with the colors of the rainbow in the sky.

Billy Learns Science

One day at school, Miss Rose was introducing the class to observation for science. Billy was very excited to learn what the class would be observing for the week. "Good morning class," Miss Rose said, "this week we will be observing the difference between hot water evaporating in a jar, versus cold water in a jar." "What is observation?" Billy asked.

"Observation is the action or process of observing something or someone carefully or in order to gain information." Miss Rose explained. "The question for the week is, which jar of water will evaporate faster, the cold water, or the hot water?"

Miss Rose split the children up in two groups. Billy was in the same group as Annie and CJ, where they were the hot water group, and the other half of students were the cold-water group.

"For the week," Miss Rose explained, "each group will mark on their jars by observing how much water is left, while being sealed tightly. Each line made will show how much water has evaporated."

Day by day, each group marked their jars. On the last day of the week, Miss Rose had the students sit together so they could discuss which jar of water evaporated. "Today we will discuss which jar of water evaporated more, the cold water or the hot water. As we can see, the hot water evaporated faster than the cold water."

Billy raised his hand. "Yes Billy?" Miss Rose said. "Why did the hot water evaporate more than the cold water?" Billy asked. "That's a great question." Miss Rose said. "The hot water evaporated faster than the cold water because of the space in between the water, which is air, that increases as the temperature of the water increases as well. For instance, if we take a cold popsicle on a stick, and sit it in the sun, will the popsicle melt or stay the same?" Miss Rose asked. "It will melt!" Billy said laughing. "The sun is really hot." "That is correct." Miss Rose said.

"Hot water and cold water are two different temperatures, but if we had both jars with either cold water or hot water, they both will evaporate the same. A second example is if you were hot because you were outside playing in the sun, how would you cool down? Would you hydrate by drinking hot water or cold water?" "Cold water." Billy answered.

"That is correct." Miss Rose said. "Cold water brings the temperature down, where as hot water brings the temperature up. So, remember students, when we fill hot because we are outside, always find something that can cool you down, and when it is cold, always find something to keep you warm."

"Like hot chocolate!!?!" Billy asked with excitement.

"Like hot chocolate." Miss Rose said with a smile.

Billy's Adventure To the Zoo

Today Billy is so excited for his class field trip to the zoo. As he enters class with his friends, Annie and CJ, they just can't help but rejoice for a day full of fun and adventure.

"I can't wait to see all the animals" Billy said with excitement. "I can't wait to see the bears, those are my favorite" said CJ. "I can't wait to see the birds," said Annie, "flamingos are my favorite. Their pink, big, and have long beaks."

As the children continued their talk about what they would love to see at the zoo, Miss Rose made an announcement.

"Hello class today is the day we will be going on our field trip to the zoo, and while we are there, we will see how animals live in their own habitat. Who's ready for an adventure?"

"We are!" said the class with joy. "Alright," she said, "let's load up on the bus, and off to the zoo we go!"

Billy got onto the bus and sat next to Annie and CJ. Once everyone was loaded up, the bus was off to take them to their adventure.

Now that the bus has made it to the entrance of the zoo, the bus was approached by the tour guide. The bus driver opened the door, to welcome her in.

"Hello little boys and girls, my name is Amy, I will be giving you a tour around the zoo today."

"Hello Amy" the class said. "Now," Amy said, "does anyone know about the animals we keep here?" Billy raised his hand. "Yes, little boy?" Amy asked. "I know there are tigers, I love tigers" Billy said. "That is correct" Amy said, "We have tigers and lions here. We have so many animals that you can think of." "Even bats?" CJ asked, "Even bats" Amy answered.

Everyone began exiting off the bus and walked in a line. The first stop was to see an alligator show. All the students took a seat. Billy sat with Annie and CJ in the front row. The first alligator that came out was a baby alligator. "Now," said Amy, "this is one of our babies, her name is Sally, she is a month old. She likes to swim in the pool with her brothers and sisters. Can anyone tell me where alligators live?" Annie raised her hand. "Yes, little girl?" Amy asked, "Alligators are in big places with water." "That is right" Amy answered, "Alligators can be seen in Southern Florida along with crocodiles. Both alligators and crocodiles live side by side in freshwater water environments such as ponds, marshes, wetlands, rivers, lakes, and swamps, and even in brackish environments."

As Amy continued to talk about the alligators, each student was able to hold baby Sally.

"She's so scaly" Billy said. "That is true" Amy replied, "as alligators begin to grow their skin becomes thick and spotted, and that is a sensory for alligators to feel and touch within their habitat."

The children were so excited about what they learned from Amy about alligators. As the tour continued, they, met many more animals and learned about their habitat. By the end of the tour Billy, Annie, and CJ saw their favorite type of animal; tigers, bears, and flamingos.

As everyone returned to the bus, everyone thanked Amy for the tour. As Billy got on the bus he turned to Annie and CJ and said, "Today was a good day for the zoo adventure."

Billy's Imagination

Billy woke up in a happy mood. "I can't wait to get to school today" he said. He brushed his teeth, got dressed, and ran down the stairs for breakfast. "Good morning Billy "said his mom, "Good morning mom!" "Well, your happy today" his mom said with a smile, "Oh yes! I can't wait to get to school to see Annie and CJ. We have so much fun together in Miss Rose class. We work together and help one another. They are good friends."

"Well then," she said, "we will eat breakfast and I will take you to school today."

As Billy's mom pulls up to the school, Billy sees Annie and CJ at the school door.

"There's CJ and Annie!" Billy said with excitement "Okay Billy," his mom said, "have a great day" "Thanks mom." Billy hurried and ran over to Annie and CJ where they were waiting for him. "Hey guys!" said Billy. "Hey Billy" said Annie. Billy's mom honked her horn and all three of the children waved good bye and went inside before the bell rang.

In class, Billy, Annie, and CJ were in front of the turtle tank playing, laughing, and having a fun time. "What do you think we will learn today?" asked Billy. "I have no idea," said CJ, "But I know it will be fun." Miss Rose walked into the room with a box of costumes and hats. "Good morning class," "Good morning Miss Rose" the class said. "Time to start our lesson, please take a seat in your spot on the rug, and let's begin. "Everyone raced to their letter, laughing and giggling with one another. Billy, Annie, and CJ were so excited to learn what Miss Rose had in stored for them.

"Today," Miss. Rose said, "we are going to learn how to use our imagination." "Imagination?" asked Billy. "Yes" said Miss Rose. "What is imagination Miss Rose?" CJ asked. "Imagination is a way that you can be who or where you want to be without actually being there. You can use your imagination by putting on a costume, playing with your toys, or even seeing the objects in your mind" Miss Rose explained. Then Miss Rose said, "In this box, I have many costumes for each of you to try on, I would like each of you to come up one at a time and pick out the one you find most fun to be."

One by one, each student picked out a costume with a hat. Billy chose the fireman, Annie chose the princess, and CJ chose the policeman. "Now that everyone has chosen a costume, Miss Rose said, "I want you all to imagine a story of what it would be like to be that person. I would like each person to come up and tell the class your imagination story." Each student came up and gave a short story of who, what, and where they were in their imagination. After CJ gave his imagination story, Billy was next. "Okay Billy," Miss Rose said, "tell the class about your imagination story."

"I am a fireman, in my imagination, I am riding in my big red truck, with my dog, helping people. I love being a fireman. I can see myself saving my neighbor's cat from a tree, and everyone is cheering and calling me a hero because I have saved the day." "That is wonderful Billy" Miss Rose said. After everyone has completed their short story, Miss Rose said, "Now that everyone has an idea of what imagination is, I want you to understand, that we all can use our imagination to be where, or what we want to be. No matter how big or how small our imagination is, we can achieve what we want in our mind, in games, or with each other. When we imagine, we can create a world of our own that we see whenever we use our imagination.

So, remember, even though right now you are small, you can always imagine yourself being who you want to be in the future."

Billy's Show
And Tell

Billy walks into class with a big smile on his face. Today was the day all the students could bring something or someone in for show and tell. Billy couldn't wait to talk about what he liked to share with the class. As the bell rang Miss Rose walked in.

"Good morning class" said Miss Rose, "Good morning Miss Rose" said the class.

"Today we will be sharing with the class what our favorite thing or person is, and I would like each person to tell the class what makes the special person or thing important to you."

Everyone could not wait to share. First up was Billy's friend Annie. "For show and tell I brought in my pet hamster. Her name is Bubbles. I've had her since she was a baby. She likes to eat seeds, carrots, and many special treats I give her. She is important to me because when I am sad she will make me happy. I love to play with her, read to her, and we even watch movies together. She is an awesome pet and I wouldn't trade her for anything else in the world."

"That is great Annie" said Miss Rose. Next, was Billy. "Okay Billy," said Miss Rose, "what have you brought in for show and tell?". Before Billy could say what, he brought in for show and tell, there was a knock on the door. As the door opened, Billy looked to see that it was his father. "You made it!" Billy said with excitement. Billy ran and gave his father a big hug. "I wouldn't miss your show and tell for anything else in this world" his father said. Billy and his father walked up to the front of the class together.

"Who is this Billy?" Miss Rose asked. "This is my father. He is an army man.

My father is important to me because he protects the world. He makes me feel safe. I look up to my father because one day, I hope to be just like him. He makes me happy, especially when we get to spend time together. He teaches me how to fish and how to fix cars. I love spending time with my father and that's why he is important to me." Everyone clapped after Billy shared his show and tell.

After everyone shared their special someone for show and tell, Miss Rose stood up and wanted to show the class her show and tell. "Now class," she said, "since you all have a special someone or something that you have shared, now I'm going to share something with you. For my show and tell I have a special treat for you all." Miss Rose pulled out a big box. In the box, Miss Rose put together baggies of treats for each student. "You all are special to me. You all make me happy to be your teacher. You all have a special place in my heart that makes me feel so happy to teach you every single day. You all make me laugh and smile, and even though I teach you, you all teach me as well. So, remember, even though we all have someone or something that is special to us that is different from one another, we can be special to someone else."

Billy's Trip Around The World

On one sunny day Miss Rose planned a special trip for her class. No one knew what kind of adventure Miss Rose had in stored for them. Billy was playing with Annie and CJ by Mindy the turtle. While everyone was having a great time, Miss Rose was outside with other kindergarten teachers preparing a wonderful outside adventure.

Back in the class, Billy, Annie, and CJ were discussing what could possibly be outside to make such a wonderful adventure.

"Do you think it's a trampoline?" asked Annie. "I don't think so" said CJ. "Maybe it's a race track." said CJ. "It could be the circus" said Billy. All the children laughed. While the children were coming up with ideas Miss Rose walked in. "Hello class" said Miss Rose, "Good morning Miss Rose" said the class. "Today we will be taking a trip around the world." "Around the world?" asked Billy, "Yes" said Miss Rose. "We will be exploring different types of cultures we have around the globe. We will identify each cultural flag."

"What is culture?" asked Billy. "Culture is the custom, art, and social interactions of a particular nation, people, or other social group" Miss Rose explained. "That sounds fun Miss Rose" said Annie. "Well then," said Miss Rose, "who's ready for a trip around the world?" "Me! Me! Me!" said the class. "Let's line up and off we go onto our adventure around the world."

All the children lined up and started off to their adventure. When they arrived at the playground, there were a lot of colors of different flags, food on tables, and many people with different clothing. "Wow" said Billy, "this is amazing." There were many other kindergarten students, so all the children paired up in groups and started off exploring each station.

Billy was in a group with Annie and CJ. The first table Billy, Annie, and CJ came across was station for Canada. "Wow" said Billy, "cool flag." "Yes" said Miss Rose, "this is Canada. Their flag has the colors red and white with the maple leaf. Here in Canada when you must go to the store, you have to drive in town to get your groceries." "In town?" asked Billy, "Yes" Miss Rose said. "Canada is a big state and unlike us who may have stores close by our homes, in Canada you have to go into town."

The children continued their adventure to see new states. They made a stop by Italy, then Mexico, Africa, China, and Australia. Later in the day Miss Rose gathered all the children together and went back to the classroom. Once back snacks were set up for the children, and Miss Rose began to summarize the lesson for the day.

"Now remember this, we are all people, we may have different ways of speaking, dressing, and socializing, but we are all the same. No matter where you come from, or where you go to visit, we can all learn from one another, no matter where you live in the world."

Billy Learns
The Time

As Billy was sitting in class, working on his coloring page, he noticed a sound that he could not seem to find. Billy raised his hand. "Yes Billy?" Miss Rose asked. "What's that sound?" he asked. "Sound?" she asked. "Yes," he said, "that sound, I can't seem to find that sound". Miss Rose looked around. "Oh, you mean that sound" and pointed to the clock on the wall. "Yes, that's it" he said. "That is the clock, it makes a ticking sound after each second has past" she explained. "The clock is also part of lesson we will learn today".

Miss Rose grabbed the clock down and placed it on her desk and began to teach her lesson on time. "Now, there are many ways to find out the time. Sometimes you can find the time on your watch, on the clock, such as the one on the wall, or anything that is electronic that has the numbers for time. The time goes by second, minutes, and hours. For instance, the clock on the wall. It has three hands: the big hand for the hour, the little hand for the minutes, and a third for the seconds" she explained. "How do you know what number the correct time is?" Billy asked. "Here, I'll show you" she said.

Miss Rose opened the clock from the wall, so Billy could see up close how the clock works. "See here," she said, "this big hand is on the number 11, and here the small hand, it's on the number 6. That means that the time right now is 11:30 in the morning". "But I don't see a 3 or a 0" Billy said. "That is correct," said Miss Rose, "this clock here is a circle and goes from 1 to 12, and those numbers are bold because they represent the hours in the day". How many hours are in a day?" Billy asked. "There are 24 hours in a day" she answered. "See here, the small hand counts the minutes. You see those little lines in the middle of each number including the lines on top of each number 1-12, those lines represent one minute. How many lines do you see together between 1 and 2?" she asked.

"I see 1,2,3,4,5. There are 5 lines between 1 and 2" he said. "That is correct" Miss Rose said, "every 5 lines, counts as 5 minutes that has past, but you have to add 5 minutes every time the small hand passes to the next 5 minutes" she explained. "Now, the third hand will be a bit longer, or a different shape then the big hand and little hand because the third hand represents the second. The sound you heard was the third hand letting us know that another second has past by. That sound is a ticking sound. Listen to the sound again and watch as each time the third hand moves" she said.

Billy watched as each time the third hand moved. "Tick. Tick. Tick." Each time the third hand moved, it made the ticking sound. "Thanks Miss Rose, you taught me a lot about the time".

After school Billy went around the house to find many objects that could have the time. He went to the kitchen, saw the clock in the kitchen window, he ran to the living room and saw the clock that stood as tall as he did. Billy was so determined to learn the time, and thanks to Miss Rose, he was becoming the best time teller ever.

Billy Learns AboutLady Bugs

One day at school, Billy was playing on the playground with his friends CJ and Annie. He was so happy to be able to run around after a wonderful learning adventure with Miss Rose. Suddenly the bell rang, and it was time to go inside to go home. As soon as Billy walked in Annie noticed a bug on his shirt. "Hey Billy, what's that bug on your shirt?" she asked. "Where?" asked Billy. Annie picked it off and showed him. "See, this bug" she said. Billy and Annie admired the little bug. It was small, red, and had black dots all around the top. "Let's go ask Miss Rose she may know" said Annie, and off they ran to class before it was time to go.

Once back in class, Billy and Annie walked up to Miss Rose to show her the little bug that landed on his shirt. "Miss Rose?" said Billy. "Yes Billy, how can I help you?" she asked. "When we were out playing Annie saw this bug on my shirt. What kind of bug is it?" he asked. "Can I take a look?" Miss Rose asked. Annie held out her hand to show Miss Rose the bug on Billy's shirt. "Oh, that is a ladybug" she said. "A ladybug?" asked Billy. "Yes, actually that is what we will talk about tomorrow for class" Miss Rose said. "Let's put this little guy in this jar, and he will be able to help me tomorrow for our lesson." Miss Rose place the lady bug in the jar with holes and place it on her desk. "I can't wait to learn about the lady bug" Billy said. The bell had rung, it was time for Billy and Annie to go home.

The next day, Billy and Annie were standing at Miss Rose desk to admire the lady bug. The bell rang, and Miss Rose walked with a box full of books and pictures. "Good morning everyone" she said. "Let's take a sit, Billy and Annie would you like to help me with today's lesson?" she asked. "Sure" they said. Billy and Annie walked to the front of the class with smiles on their faces. "Yesterday, Billy and Annie were playing outside. When coming in Annie noticed a little bug on Billy's shirt. A lady bug" she said. Miss Rose grabbed the jar with the lady bug and showed the class. "Today's lesson is about lady bugs."

Miss Rose had Billy and Annie pass out pictures and books to each student. "Now, lady bugs can come in many different colors as you can see in the pictures. You may have seen them around your home or sitting on flowers. The good thing is that lady bugs will not harm you. They are beautiful to see during the time it's warm outside" she explained. "What color is this lady bug?" Billy asked. "This lady bug is orange" she answered. "Lady bugs can be other colors such as blue, black, gray, and even pink. They love being around flowers because that is their source for food". "That is amazing" said Billy. "How would you guys like to put this lady bug outside by the flower garden?" asked Miss Rose. "I think that's a great idea" said Billy. Miss Rose took the class by the garden to place the lady bug on it's new home.

When the class approached the garden, they noticed a lot more than just a place to give the lady bug a home. There were more lady bugs flying around the flowers. "This must have been the lady bugs home!" said Billy. Billy and the rest of his classmates were amazed by the different color lady bugs. Miss Rose opened the jar, scooped the lady bug, and place it on a flower. As soon as the lady bug realized it was outside, it flew off the flower and landed back on Billy's shirt. "I guess this lady bug really likes me" he said. "I guess so" Miss Rose replied. Billy placed the lady bug back on the flower. "I'll call you Lady" he said. He smiled and off the class went back to class.

After school Billy ran inside to grab his dad's magnifying glass and, in the backyard, to find more lady bugs just like his new friend Lady.

Billy Goes Camping

One afternoon, Billy was playing with his toys in his room. While he was playing his dad walks in. "Hey Billy" said his dad, "Hey dad!" said Billy. "How would you like to go camping today?" his dad asked. "Camping? What's camping?" Billy asked. "Camping is where we sleep in tents, sit by a camp fire, eat smores, tell great stories, and look at the stars at night" his dad explained. "That sounds like fun!" Billy said excitingly. "Let's do it!"

Billy followed his dad outside to the back yard. Outside Billy saw that his dad setup everything they would need for camping. "We are going to set the tent up together" his dad said. "How do we do that?" Billy asked. "First, we have to put the poles in the loops, so the tent can form its shape, which will make room for me and you" his dad explained. Billy helped his dad put each pole in the loops. "Next, we will place the stakes on each corner so that the tent can stay where we want it. After that, the tent will be complete."

Once the tent was complete, Billy was ready for the next task. He watched as his dad setup the wood to make a camp fire for later when the sun went down. Next, Billy and his dad enjoyed a wonderful meal of hot dogs, chips, lemonade, and popsicles for dessert, and sharing jokes to make each other laugh.

As the sun went down, Billy's dad set the campfire. Once the fire was lit, his dad brought blankets, so they could admire the stars. "Now we are going to make smore sandwiches" Billy's dad said. "How will we do that?" Billy asked. "First, we take a marshmallow, and put them on a stick. Next, we get a graham cracker for the base of the sandwich and take a piece of chocolate and place it on top of the cracker. Then we take the marshmallow on the stick and place it over the camp fire. Once you see the marshmallow turn brown it's ready to be placed on top of the chocolate, and then we add another graham cracker on top to complete the sandwich."

While Billy and his dad were eating their sandwiches, they admired the stars, and the full moon. Suddenly, they hear crickets. "Chirp! Chirp! Chirp! Chirp!". "I love hearing the crickets" Billy said. "Do you know why they make that noise?" his dad asked. "Not. At. All." Billy said. "It is because that is how crickets communicate with one another. Sometimes it could be in the day, or at night" his dad explained.

After listening to more stories, Billy was ready for bed. He got into the tent and slipped into his sleeping bag. Before going to sleep Billy said, "I love camping dad, I wish we could do this forever." "Don't worry Billy," he said, "we will have many more camping trips such as this."

Billy's Planting Project

One morning at school, Billy walks into class to find cups on their tables filled with dirt. "I wonder what these are for" he said. "I think we are going to grow something" said Annie, "my mom uses cups like these all the time to put her seeds in, so they can start to grow". The bell rang, and Miss Rose came in with a small bag of seeds. "Good morning class" Miss Rose said. "Good morning Miss Rose" said the class. "I know you may be wondering what the cups are for today. We will be learning how to plant and grow our very on beans". Billy was so excited to be able to learn how to go his very plant.

Miss Rose gave each student a tray that had six cups to place each seed in to plant. Billy gently carefully poured the dirt in each cup. Then, he gently placed one seed in each cup with dirt covered the seeds. Once everyone completed planting their seeds Miss Rose took them to the garden room where the seeds could get plenty of sun and be able to get watered by the students.

Everyday Miss Rose took the students back and forth to care for the seeds, and each day Billy couldn't wait to see how his seeds came out. "I hope it comes out as big as me" he said. The following week Miss Rose took the children to the garden room to see that their beans have sprouted. "Wow, it has a green leaf" Billy said. "Yes," said Miss Rose, "this is the sprouting stage where the beans will show that they are growing. With you all taking care of them so well, by providing sunlight, water, and room to grow, they will come out into wonderful beans".

Billy went home with such pride and joy because he took such good care of his seeds. Suddenly he came up with an idea, "I could help mommy in her garden". Off he went outside to help his mother in the garden, to learn more about gardening.

Billy Learns His Shapes

From learning many different subjects and doing many projects Billy loved to learn new things in class. For the morning lesson Miss Rose was teaching the class about their shapes. "Today we will be working with blocks and identifying each shape" she said. Each shape was drawn on the board with the word next to each picture. "The first picture is a circle, find a block in the group that looks just like a circle" Miss Rose said. Next there was a triangle, after that a square, and a star. Billy was so happy to understand what shapes were. After school Billy practiced his shapes with his mom and dad. They were so proud him, and Billy was proud too.

Billy's Last
Day Of School

Billy was so excited for the last day of school. His mom and dad planned his summer vacation. "I can't wait to get to school" he said to his mother. As his mother pulls in to the school Billy sees Annie and CJ. "Have a good day dear" said his mom. "Thanks mom" said Billy. Billy ran to Annie and CJ, so they could walk together to class. In class, Billy couldn't wait to talk to his friends about the summer. "My dad said we are going to go fishing" he said, "my mom said were going out of town to see my grandma" said Annie, "my dad is going take me to a baseball game" said CJ. They couldn't wait until the summer started. Suddenly Miss Rose walked in the room.

"Hello class, I see everyone is ready for the summer time" she said. Everyone was giggling and laughing because today was the last day. "Don't worry Miss Rose, we will see you again when the summer is over, right? We will be in your class again" said Billy. "Yes, you will see me, but you will be in first grade" she said. "But you will be our teacher, right?" asked Annie. "You all will have a new teacher" Miss Rose said. "You all have been wonderful students, you've learned so much from me this year. We've laughed, went on adventures, became friends, and learned from one another. Next school year you all will move up to the first grade and learn from another teacher who will teach you more, about the world of education. Don't worry, you can always come see me when you like, or even just passing by. But remember, you will always learn something new from a wonderful teacher who comes with joy and happiness of teaching you".

After completing the last day of school, Billy stood outside with Annie and CJ. "I'm glad to know you both and have such good friends like you" Billy said. "Don't worry Billy," CJ said, "we will see each other again". Billy hugged Annie and CJ before saying good bye. "Today starts a great summer" said Billy, and off he went to start his wonderful adventure for the summer.

My Pets
and Their
Personalities

My pets have personalities and show them each day. When I come home, they greet me in a different way.

First there is Angel, my grandma's dog that she loves. She barks so loud I could hear her, when I come in the door. She likes to sit in the sun on a pillow, I really don't know why, but she enjoys it, and so do I.

Next there is Sadie, she's such a big dog, she loves to go on car rides, and feel the breeze in the air. She loves when we have campfires, especially when we roast hot dogs. She loves to get a treat, when she is such a good dog.

Then we have Myrtle, she is such a good turtle. She loves to watch T.V., and swims happy when mommy's home. She gets excited for her favorite fruits, strawberries, and watermelon.

Of course, we have two cats, Kyrie and Bandit, but like the others, they have their own personalities, just as I said.

Kyrie loves to lounge around, and sleep all day, but when it comes to feeding time, she comes right away.

As for Bandit, she is sneaky, and that is every day. She will take your straws and play with them, and even hide them in the bed.

All my pets have a personality, I'm so happy their mine. They may be different, but to me, they are one of a kind.

Printed in the United States
By Bookmasters